£5,99

**GETTING
CRITICAL**

POCKET STUDY SKILLS

Series Editor: **Kate Williams**, *Oxford Brookes University, UK*
Illustrations by Sallie Godwin

For the time-pushed student, the *Pocket Study Skills* pack a lot of advice into a little book. Each guide focuses on a single crucial aspect of study giving you step-by-step guidance, handy tips and clear advice on how to approach the important areas which will continually be at the core of your studies.

Published

14 Days to Exam Success
Blogs, Wikis, Podcasts and More
Brilliant Writing Tips for Students
Completing Your PhD
Doing Research
Getting Critical
Planning Your Essay
Planning Your PhD
Reading and Making Notes
Referencing and Understanding Plagiarism
Reflective Writing
Report Writing
Science Study Skills
Studying with Dyslexia
Success in Groupwork
Time Management
Writing for University

Pocket Study Skills
Series Standing Order
ISBN 978–0230–21605–1
(outside North America only)

You can receive future titles in this series as they are published by placing a standing order. Please contact your bookseller or, in case of difficulty, write to us at the address below with your name and address, the title of the series and the ISBN quoted above.

Customer Services Department, Macmillan Distribution Ltd, Houndmills, Basingstoke, Hampshire RG21 6XS, England

POCKET STUDY SKILLS

Kate Williams

GETTING
CRITICAL

palgrave
macmillan

First published 2009 by
PALGRAVE MACMILLAN

Palgrave Macmillan in the UK is an imprint of Macmillan Publishers Limited, registered in England, company number 785998, of Houndmills, Basingstoke, Hampshire RG21 6XS.

Palgrave Macmillan in the US is a division of St Martin's Press LLC, 175 Fifth Avenue, New York, NY 10010.

Palgrave Macmillan is the global academic imprint of the above companies and has companies and representatives throughout the world.

Palgrave® and Macmillan® are registered trademarks in the United States, the United Kingdom, Europe and other countries

ISBN-13: 978-0-230-58476-1
ISBN-10: 0-230-58476-4

This book is printed on paper suitable for recycling and made from fully managed and sustained forest sources. Logging, pulping and manufacturing processes are expected to conform to the environmental regulations of the country of origin.

A catalogue record for this book is available from the British Library.

10 9 8 7 6 5 4 3
19 18 17 16 15 14 13 12 11

Printed in China

Contents

Acknowledgements   vi
Introduction   vii

Part 1 Getting a critical mindset   1
1 Getting strategic   1
2 The language of assessment   7
3 The stairway to critical thinking   12

Part 2 Getting critical in research and reading   17
4 A critical approach to reading lists   19
5 A critical search online   22
6 To read or not to read? A critical decision   26
7 Reading it: tips for reading and notes   29
8 But is it any good? Evaluating (web) sources   32

9 A critical record of reading: an annotated bibliography   37

Part 3 Getting critical in writing   43
10 Answer the question!   44
11 Writing paragraphs: a critical skill   49
12 The 'critical' bit in essays and assignments   61

Part 4 Critical steps   69
13 Stepping up the stairway to critical thinking   70
14 Frameworks to help critical analysis   77
15 Becoming a writer   88
Appendix   89
References   91
Useful sources   93
Index   95

Acknowledgements

A big thank you to the many people who have contributed to this guide. First, thanks to the students who have discussed their dilemmas and shared their 'Eureka!' moments with me over the years. Special thanks to Aline, Tom, Yiannis and Adrienne for permission to use extracts from their work. This guide brings key points from these private conversations to a wider audience.

Special thanks too to Hazel Rothera for advice on online searching; to Mary Woolliams, Dan Butcher and Jim Pye, who contributed to my thoughts on critical thinking as we worked on a guide for Health and Social Care students; to Berry O'Donovan for permission to draw on the framework for assessment used in the Business School at Oxford Brookes University and to colleagues at Upgrade where 'critical thinking' is much discussed.

Thanks too to Sallie Godwin for turning my scribbles into witty sketches.

The author and publishers wish to thank the following for permission to reproduce copyright material: Open University for 'Critical thinking' from their website; Elsevier for the article by Osborne and Kiker.

Introduction

> *Your account is too descriptive ...*

> *You need to show more analysis in your work ...*

> *You need to question the findings in more detail ...*

> *You need to be more critical ...*

If you have ever had feedback like this on your work and wondered what it means, why it matters and what you should do about it, then this guide is for you.

The guide has been written to show students:

- what being 'critical' means in higher education
- how to bring that 'critical' dimension into all aspects of your work.

Being 'critical' at university

The word 'critical' has several meanings in everyday life, most commonly:

- finding fault: a negative comment such as *not good enough*; *sloppily done*; *could do better*; *why didn't you …?*
- key, decisive, crucial: – as in '*a critical moment*', '*critically ill*', '*a critical decision*'.

Neither of these is the meaning of 'critical' when describing the quality tutors want to see in students' work. 'Critical' in university work means being thoughtful, asking questions, not taking things you read (or hear) at face value. It means finding information and understanding different approaches and using them in your writing.

A critical approach is not a form of writing in itself (like an essay or report), nor a particular 'hat' you put on from time to time when you read, or an optional add-on. It is a mindset you need for life and work, and very much part of the wider picture of having a methodical and thoughtful approach to your studies. When you find your own questioning 'critical' approach (and you will!), you and your studies will take off.

Being 'critical': why does it matter?

Consider these mini scenarios: why does being 'critical' matter in each?

Scenario 1

You like the wind in your hair. It is really worth wearing a cycle helmet? Of course you know the advice is to wear one, but you need convincing. What evidence underpins this recommendation? Is it the outcome of systematic research by people who have:

- treated head injuries
- studied accident statistics
- done this in several settings, by methods set out clearly
- and reached the conclusions which led to this recommendation?

And do you change your behaviour? That's your choice!

The 'critical' bit? When specialists – or you – study the studies, they need to 'think critically' about the quality of the evidence, and the way the studies were carried out. The conclusions are only as good as the methods.

Scenario 2

Students are set essays to discuss concepts and ideas, like 'Discuss the proposition that *The Heart of Darkness* is a racist novel'.
Why?

▶ The author, Joseph Conrad, was influential in his time and today.
▶ Racism is a complex issue, and simplistic answers do nothing to address it.
▶ Current social attitudes have evolved from past attitudes, so to understand the present, we need to understand how we got here.

The 'critical' bit? You read the book thoughtfully to understand Conrad's attitudes. You ask questions about when and how the concept of 'racism' developed, relate it to him and his time, and reach a conclusion. The question matters because concepts shape societies and individuals' experiences within them.

The 'critical' bit? This practitioner – the teacher – has knowledge and understanding, and is able to apply it. She reflects and thinks about the individual child to evaluate what is going well and not so well, and to develop her approach accordingly.

All these situations show a 'critical' awareness. This dimension informs policies, decisions and actions; attitudes and awareness; professional good practice – and more. It is an essential quality to bring to life and work.

So what's new?

Not a lot. You are naturally critical most of the time. You know that (some) newspaper reports only give half the story; that 'buy one, get one free' in one supermarket is still more expensive than the straight price in another; that you'd go and see a film one friend recommends, and steer clear of someone else's recommendations. You discriminate, make judgements, set one view against another, and ultimately take responsibility for your own judgements and actions.

All you've got to do is to carry this over into your studies. You are not a sponge, soaking up knowledge, and squeezing it out in your assignments to prove you 'know' it. You entered university as a thoughtful and questioning person, and your course is an opportunity for you to develop these qualities in a new context.

About this guide

This guide is about how you *do* this:

Part 1: Getting a critical mindset is about understanding the language of the guidance you are given about your essays and assignments, and understanding how your work is assessed.

Part 2: Getting critical in research and reading is about bringing this critical mindset to your reading lists, your own online searching, and record keeping.

Part 3: Getting critical in writing takes a methodical look at the key processes in writing an essay or assignment, with lots of examples.

Part 4: Critical steps is for dipping into. It takes a closer look at the meaning of words used to describe critical analysis, and at how you might use a 'framework'.

Kate Williams

Order No:

Class:

Accession No:

Type:

PART 1

GETTING A CRITICAL MINDSET

1 Getting strategic

This section takes a good look at how to get that critical mindset in your studies. It starts asking questions right from the beginning.

Six **strategic questions** are used by many people to get themselves started in tackling a task, whether it's planning a project, getting to grips with reading, or writing something:

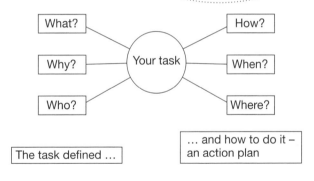

What?	How?
Why?	Your task	When?
Who?	Where?

The task defined ...

... and how to do it – an action plan

Finding the answers to these key questions will help to keep you alert and critical. Try it first in relation to a course handbook.

A strategic reading of a course handbook!

Course handbooks are an essential source of guidance. They tell you what you have to do, and often quite a lot about how to set about it, as well as the practicalities like when it needs to be done by.

Your critical approach to your studies starts here! Read your handbook carefully and check online to make sure you have all the information you need to answer the strategic questions.

The task defined

The first three key questions (on the left in the table) will help you to get the measure of the task(s) you have been set.

What exactly do you have to produce?	... in your next essay/ assignment?
What format? Essay? Report? Specific format? Presentation? Tests?	
Any guidance about structure, layout and style?	
How long?	
What % marks does the task count for?	
What topic(s)?	

Why are you being asked to do this?	
External reasons: the 'learning outcomes' you are expected to achieve.	
Internal reasons: your private purpose – interest in the subject, personal satisfaction.	

Who are you writing for? It helps you write if you can visualise your reader.	
Your tutor is always your audience. What do you know about what s/he wants to see?	
Do you have another real audience, for example giving a presentation to your seminar group?	
Or an imagined audience, like writing a report (for a company for example), or an article for a particular journal?	

Most writing tasks do not specify an audience (beyond the obvious – your tutor or a colleague). You may find it helpful to imagine a 'default' audience when you write.

Write as if …

… you are addressing someone with the same experience and knowledge of the general subject area as yourself, but who has not yet covered this particular topic/module/course. If you do this you will not be tempted to:

▶ talk up, using fancy language designed to impress
▶ talk down, with an inappropriate informal or chatty style.

Talk on the level, using clear, simple language; use short sentences; and draw on the specialist language, conventions and style of your subject when you need to.

And how to do it – an action plan

How …? What guidance are you given about what to include?	… in your next essay/ assignment?
For example: Use of appendices? Style of referencing? Acceptable and unacceptable practice?	

When …? is the deadline for the final hand-in?	
Are there earlier deadlines for drafts and various elements?	
How will you balance working towards one deadline with working towards others? And life, job etc.?	

Where …? will you find the information?	
How much of it is easy to find (course readers, textbooks, special collections)?	
How much do you have to research yourself? And go beyond the reading list?	

Your answers to these questions will help you work out an action plan for getting it done. You may like to try some of these suggestions:

- Complete a term or semester timeline (see the template on p89).
- List the specifics: break down major tasks from the timeline into small tasks.
- Check your diary – for job schedules, weekends away, a social life even …
- Plan your week: look for short start-up slots, longer working chunks, short review slots.
- Write 'to do' lists (make each item a small one!), and tick them off when you have done them.

For more suggestions, see *Time Management* in this series.

Now take a closer look at the specific guidance you have been given about what tutors are looking for in what you write, and how it will be assessed. This is where you get to grips with the language of assessment – which at first glance can appear rather a **critical soup** …

These phrases come from the assessment criteria for an 'A' grade from a range of subject areas in a number of universities. You will notice that *critical analysis, evaluation, thinking* are words consistently linked with higher grades:

> *Good example of critical thinking in looking at the issue from more than one perspective.* (B+)

And the lack of that critical dimension often explains a lower grade:

> *What are the implications of this word? Try to be more critical in your reading.* (C)

The language of assessment   7

Assessment criteria: what are they looking for?

Tutors are often better at placing a piece of work in a particular grade than at articulating why they did it. Assessment criteria are an attempt both to express the intellectual qualities tutors are looking for, and to explain their subsequent grading.

Assessment criteria take many forms: some describe the qualities of each grade in a paragraph; others set them out as a grid (as below). Some are specific to each assignment or essay; others are generic – used across a course, department, Faculty or School. Whatever they look like, you need to look at them and quiz them before you start.

Example 1: Qualities + grading

In this style of sheet the qualities (or 'criteria') are listed on the left, and grades, set out in various ways, head the columns. It gives you a checklist of what the marker will be looking for.

Try turning assessment criteria into a checklist for yourself by answering the questions about what each phrase means.

Criteria/ qualities	A	B+	B	C	F
Knowledge and understanding Level of subject knowledge Able to identify key debates Understands relevant concepts and theory					
Evidence and analysis Logical development of argument Evaluation of source material Evidence provided to support case					
Reading and research Selection of appropriate material Effective use of a wide range of material Evidence of independent research					
Presentation Clarity of expression Clear and accurate referencing					

In your next assignment ...

What are the key debates?

What concepts and theories should you know about? Which are relevant to this question?

In one sentence, what are you going to say? What points do you want to make?

How do the various things you have read support the points you want to make? Or not?

What does 'wide range' mean? How many sources? What sort?

... going beyond the reading list

How will you tackle the reading? And pick and choose what you use and what you don't?

Example 2: Qualities defined

This style of feedback sheet is longer (often several pages), and aims to define more precisely what the grade means in relation to each quality or criterion. You need a focus when you look at these pages: study the 'A' grade criteria to see what the marker is looking for.

In these extracts, only 'Intellectual skills' is shown.

	Knowledge and understanding	Reading and research	**Intellectual skills**	Presentation
70+ A			Develops coherent, logical and relevant <u>arguments</u>, drawing appropriate <u>conclusions</u>. Demonstrates depth of critical <u>analysis</u> and independent <u>thought</u>.	

Argument again – clearly a top of the tree quality. You can only work out an argument when you have done the foundations - read, understood, - and worked with it - thought and planned.

Must have a good conclusion. Note the 's'. Several strands drawn together.

Really understanding what the articles say, how they support each other, how they differ – and showing you see this ... Hm...

Your own perspective... and evidence for it....

Look at the lower grades to see what you need to go beyond.

60–69 B+			Well-developed argument. Demonstrates independent thought and critical analysis.		*Setting out brief summaries of what you have read, even when you relate them to each other, will get you a basic pass.*
50–59 B			Develops some arguments. Demonstrates critical thinking in a straightforward manner.		
40–49 C			Assembles and links ideas.		*Simply setting down what you have read, done or heard without comment is not enough..*
Fail, resit etc.			Development of argument is weak and/or a purely descriptive account throughout. Conclusions inappropriate or absent. Unsubstantiated claims based on anecdotes/generalisations.		*Conclusions must flow from the rest of the writing.*

The description of the qualities expected in students' work will of course vary from subject to subject, tutor to tutor, one university to another. There will, however, be a consistent core of shared values and definitions of what markers expect to see.

You need evidence which itself is well founded for the statements you make.

There is no shortage of definitions and attempts to describe the qualities associated with critical thinking.[1] A definition is a good place to start when you are trying to understand something, and useful here to see what assessment criteria are based on.

The diagram opposite sets out the 'stairway' to critical thinking as described by the Open University (2008). In it you will recognise some of the terms used in assessment criteria and throughout this guide.

Start at the bottom. The first four steps suggest approaches to getting to grips with your reading and research. Your writing task may ask you to record this: *describe, analyse, compare.* The top four steps show some of the key functions you are asked to do in your writing – some of these may appear in your essay title: *evaluate, apply, justify.* These terms are considered in more detail in Chapter 13 (Part 4).

Tick all the processes you think you will have to do for your next assignment, and highlight the words and phrases that appear in the assessment criteria.

---

1 See 'Useful sources' for additional sources and brief comments.

The stairway to critical thinking

						Justify
Use critical thinking to develop arguments, draw conclusions, make inferences and identify implications.						
Transfer the understanding you have gained from your critical evaluation and use in response to questions, assignments and projects.					Apply	
Assess the worth of an idea in terms of its relevance to your needs, the evidence on which it is based and how it relates to other pertinent ideas.				Evaluate		
Bring together different sources to serve an argument or idea you are constructing. Make logical connections between the different sources that help you shape and support your ideas.			Synthesise			
		Compare	Explore the similarities and differences between the ideas you are reading about.			
	Analyse	Examine how these key components fit together and relate to each other.				
Start here ☺	Understand	Comprehend the key points, assumptions, arguments and evidence presented.				
Process	Take in the information, i.e. what you have read, heard, seen or done.					

Source: Open University (2008)

Definitions are not enough!

Of course, definitions alone are not enough to offer useful guidance about what you need to *do* to get that critical dimension into your work. Examples, models, outlines, conversation and discussion (and this book of course!) all help to translate the abstract definition into a practical understanding of what you need to put on the page.

And note …

Not every piece of work requires you to be operating on the top steps for an 'A' grade. Sometimes you will be asked to 'describe', 'trace', 'explain', and it will be possible to get an 'A' grade for it because the process is exceptionally complex, difficult, hard to disentangle. Here it is key for you to demonstrate your understanding. In essays and assignments, however, there is a correlation between the top, middle and lower steps, and the top, middle and lower grades. (See *Planning Your Essay* in this series.)

So, how do I get critical?

That critical quality will grow out of a methodical and thoughtful approach to your work. A bit like this:

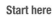

Start here

Understand what you need to
▸ do
▸ know and understand

Become a writer

Talk to your reader. Make it easy for them to follow from start to finish. Let your voice, your own style, show through in what you write.

Grow your ideas

What is the question or assignment task asking?
Do an outline plan. Locate your reading in your plan. Search for your own reading.
Look for connections.
Give yourself time.
Discuss your ideas with other students.
Find your argument.

Foundations

Choose your reading. First a general text for an overview. Then chapters and articles: read abstracts, boxes, intros and conclusions first. Make notes on what you read and where it came from.

GETTING CRITICAL IN RESEARCH AND READING

> *I can't read all that!*

A critical approach to reading starts before you have read anything …

Reading lists can be daunting. If the list you are looking at is longer than one side, you can be sure you are not expected to read everything on it for one assignment or standard essay. Think of it as suggestions from which you compile your own reading list. Your list will consist of:

- **core** materials you really do need to read from week to week to keep on top of your course and contribute to discussions
- **further** reading which will enable you understand some of the complexities; and some
- **off-list items** you have found yourself as you pursue an interest.

This mix will ensure you are getting the 'wide range' of source material that underpins the higher grades.

Textbooks are helpful in mapping the territory outlining the knowledge areas you need. They may also point out or describe areas of debate and discussion. For the debate itself, or specific studies that draw specific conclusions or develop an argument, you need to read journal articles.

So you need to have an idea about what each item is likely to offer as a basis for selecting what to read. You can tell a lot about a source just by thinking about the information in the reference.

Below (on the left) are extracts from the reading lists of specific modules, and (on the right) what you can tell about each source before you put it on your list.

Healthcare module:

On the reading list	What to expect?
Montague SE, Watson R and Herbert RA (2005). *Physiology for Nurses*, 3rd edition. London: Elsevier.	A general nursing textbook. Good for core knowledge. Check to see if there is a more recent edition.
Devendra D, Lui E and Eisenbarth G (2004). Type I diabetes: recent developments. *British Medical Journal*. l3:28, 750–54.	A journal article (four pages). The BMJ is published by the doctors' professional organisation (the BMA) so it will be well researched and reliable. This looks like a 'review' of recent research useful for healthcare practitioners. In the 'further' category.
Burden M (2003). Diabetes: signs, symptoms and making a diagnosis. *Nursing Times*. 99:1, 30–32.	A three-page article from a practitioner journal. Will be directly relevant to nursing practice. It looks 'core'.

On the reading list	What to expect?
Diabetes UK website: www.diabetes.org.uk/home.htm *Note*: This points you to a source, so does not include the details you would need to reference material from it.	A key and authoritative website in the field. Will contain a variety of material; probably good for current facts and figures (check dates of pages). Core.

Sustainable development module:

On the reading list	What to expect?
McGregor D (2002). Climate, environment and development. In Desai V and Potter RB (eds) *The companion to development studies*. London: Arnold.	A chapter in an edited book – itself on the reading list. Looks like a good intro. At a guess, 10–15 pages? Core.
UNFAO (2005). *Global forest resources assessment.* Available at http://www.fao.org/forestry/1191/en/ Note: Add the date you accessed it in your reference if you used it.	An authoritative website (United Nations). Will be a good source for up-to-date stats and trends. Core.
Mather AS and Needle CL (2000). The relationship of population and forest land. *The Geographical Journal.* 166:1, 2–13.	An article (11 pages) of peer-reviewed[2] research. Further.

Feeling less panicky? At a closer look, reading lists often turn out to be less alarming than at first glance. The same text is referred to several times for different chapters; articles turn out to be really quite short; and careful use of good websites will take you to reader-friendly material, or at least well-structured sources where you can quickly find what you want.

---

2 Every article in a 'peer reviewed' journal has been checked by specialists in the specific research area before publication.

This section is about going beyond your reading list, beyond Google, or even Google Scholar. There is a huge world of research on just about everything under the sun out there at your fingertips. But how to find what you need, now? When you know what you are looking for (something closely related to a coursework topic, or your reading list), this is probably fairly straightforward – with a little help from your friendly library. But when you are thinking about a wide-open topic – such as a possible dissertation topic – you need to use databases, and get thinking. Critically of course, perhaps a bit like this:

You – the researcher
You're interested in carbon offsetting. It is a fairly recent area of research and there's not much on it in books. You follow the library handout on searching databases and …

???!!! Help! Where do I start? There's so much stuff …

Your friendly library ☺
SEARCH FOR

| carbon offsetting |

Search Results
1147 records for 1973–2010

Start thinking. What exactly do you want to explore in your dissertation? What question are you asking? This is far too general; it isn't asking a question and you can't research it. So focus down; narrow your field of interest. Ask a question.

I'm interested in deforestation too. I've seen wildlife programmes showing the impact. I'm interested in sub-Saharan Africa: so many problems that make survival so difficult for so many and here in the West even I can't resist a cheap flight …

So how about this for a question?
What is the effect of carbon offsetting on deforestation in sub-Saharan Africa?

Your friendly library ☺
SEARCH FOR

| deforestation |

| AND | | carbon offsetting |

| AND | | sub-Saharan Africa |

Search Results
0 records found

??!! Help! There's nothing on my topic!

No. There probably isn't. This is very specific. But before you give up, go and see your friendly subject librarian, who may help you find other sources, suggest other keywords. But if there really isn't anything? This could be great if you are engaged in original fieldwork research, but if you're not ...? You need to try a two-pronged approach. Think laterally! Critically!

First try locating research on an aspect of the issue I know is well established.

Your friendly library
SEARCH FOR

deforestation

| AND | sub-Saharan Africa |

Search Results
17 records found ...

This is beginning to look researchable (migrant land rights / carbon storage in forestry / gorillas and armed conflict / cooking stoves ...) – but how to find out if there is a link with carbon offsetting?

There must be something on carbon offsetting AND deforestation in other parts of the world – or what's the debate about?

Your friendly library
SEARCH FOR

deforestation

| AND | carbon offsetting |

Search Results
51 records found ...

... many relating to South America, South East Asia ... but might something here apply to sub-Saharan Africa? And if not why not? This is getting interesting ...

At this point you will be thinking critically about what you have found and making decisions about whether this precise topic is right for you, and whether this article is useful for your topic. It could be that it is not: it might be too unknown, perfect for a PhD student who is in a position to carry out research to fill a gap in knowledge – but not for you, now.

However, by finding out what research is out there, you may have stumbled across a topic that really grabs your interest, that relates to your previous general interest with a slight shift in focus, and that you can really engage with. Or you move up a level, and locate your question in the comfort zone in the middle. Only you can decide, but, having got this far, your decision will be based on sound – critical – thinking.

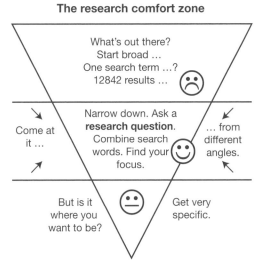

The research comfort zone

What's out there?
Start broad …
One search term …?
12842 results …

Come at it …

Narrow down. Ask a **research question**.
Combine search words. Find your focus.

… from different angles.

But is it where you want to be?

Get very specific.

6 To read or not to read? A critical decision

You find an article that looks promising, and here's the abstract. Use the strategic questions on p. 1 as a basic checklist to help you decide if it is worth reading the full text. A critical approach to reading – before you read – will save you a lot of time and effort.

Carbon offsets as an economic alternative to large-scale logging: a case study in Guyana

Tracey Osborne[a], 📝, ✉ and Clyde Kiker[b]

[a]Energy and Resources Group, University of California Berkeley, 310 Barrows Hall, Berkeley CA 94720, USA

[b]Food and Resource Economics Department, University of Florida, PO Box 110240, Gainesville, FL 32611, USA

Received 8 July 2002; revised 14 June 2004; accepted 18 June 2004. Available online 2 February 2005.

When was it published? (2005). When was the research carried out? (probably 2001-2).

What is it about? A case study will be a detailed study in a particular setting.

Where was this research carried out? Could it have any relevance to my interest in Africa?

Who are the researchers? Do they look qualified to carry out credible research? Click on the icon to find out more about how the article has (or has not) been used by other researchers.

Abstract

The <u>objective</u> of this study is to analyze the economic viability of carbon-offset projects that avoid logging in Guyana's forests. The <u>results</u> of this case study illustrate the cost effectiveness of alternative land-use options that reduce deforestation and associated greenhouse gas (GHG) emissions. This <u>analysis</u> demonstrates that using Guyana's rainforests for climate change mitigation can generate <u>equivalent</u> revenue to that of conventional large-scale logging without detrimental environmental impacts. At a 12% discount rate, the break-even price for carbon is estimated to be about US$ 0.20/tC. This estimate falls toward the low range of carbon prices for existing carbon offset <u>projects</u> that avoid deforestation.

Keywords: Carbon offsets; Deforestation; Climate change mitigation; Land use change and forestry; Guyana

Why was the research carried out? What is the aim?

What did they find out? And conclude?

How did they do it? You'd have to read the full article to find this out, and you would only do this if it is directly relevant to you.

So what ... are the wider implications of the research?

How might this research be useful to other projects? And of course to me. NOW?

Source: Reprinted from *Ecological Economics*, Volume 52, Issue 4 (1 March 2005), pp. 481–96 with permission from Elsevier.

OK. You decide that interesting though it is, it does not get close enough to your interest – which is shifting anyway towards one of the other related areas you came across earlier. So don't read it! Move on.

You're not a sponge taking it all in, reading from start to finish. As a critical reader, think of yourself as a hook, looking for relevant information to fish out, or a razor cutting through the details looking for the main points. It is your right, your decision, *not* to read – which is every bit as important as the decision to read!

When you do read, read economically – and critically, of course. Focus on the specific reading you have decided really is important and relevant to your research.

Tips for reading

Before you start ask … **why** am I reading this text? What do I want to get out of it?

I want to …

Then get a feel for it …

Survey the text critically. Note:

Title	Subtitle	Blurb	Author(s)	Date of publication	Contents (for overview) Index (for specifics)

Get an overview. Look for and read:

Abstract (article) Or chapter summary – beginning or end	Headings of subsections	Boxes and diagrams	First sentence of paragraphs

And now **read in detail** only what you have to, to get what you want out of it.

This critical approach will speed up your reading, and when you get to the detailed read you will be able to see where it fits in the bigger picture – a critical skill!

Making notes

Note making from your reading is an incredibly important process. 'Process' is the right word, because it is when you make notes that your brain processes the information. It goes in as new information (data, explanation or argument), and down on your page as something you now know, understand, want to remember, and plan to use as you get to grips with your topic. You start off not knowing or understanding something, and end up knowing and understanding. That's great!

This is where you need to be careful. University education sets a high store by knowledge – which, if you like, is the core product of universities. An essential part of joining the academic community (which as a student you have done) is to be respectful of this knowledge (or argument, or explanation or whatever), and of the people who generated it or set it down. So record your sources meticulously.

Try to keep track of this separateness in your notes. Try to capture:
▶ the key points, key phrases of your source, and where it comes from
▶ your own thoughts, observations and connections. This is where you 'stand on the shoulders' of researchers and thinkers who have gone before.

Tips for note making	Why?
Record each source, the full reference,[3] so you know where ideas or findings come from:	▶ so your reader can find it ▶ to avoid retracing your steps later ▶ to get credit for the work you have done ▶ to give credit to authors for the work they have done.
Note key points relevant to your purpose	... to focus on what *you* want to get out of the text, not necessarily the same main points or order as the author.
Use colours, spacing, bullets, diagrams, arrows, sketches – whatever helps you understand the text. Go easy on the highlighter ... try a pencil.	Change the format of the original to reflect how you are making sense of the information. A highlighter highlights – usually too much and you can't undo it!
Avoid writing full sentences	... to leave yourself free to grasp the idea, not get bogged down in the words of the writer.
Don't copy, except for short phrases you may want to use as quotes	... so the wording of your notes is your own except where you can see from the quote marks and page number that they are not.
Leave lots of space, and experiment with styles till you find what suits you	... so you can add detail later.
Check back quickly with the original	... to make sure you haven't missed anything crucial.

3 For more on referencing, see *Referencing and Understanding Plagiarism* in this series.

But is it any good? Evaluating (web) sources

'Evaluation' is something you do all the time, automatically. Look at what it means – see the word 'value' in the middle of '**evalu**ate'. What is the value of this? As research? As a source of information? To me, for my present purpose?

The web is open to anyone, and that is great. But it is 'buyer beware' in the use you make of it. The explosion of information we all have access to in a click means there are no gatekeepers to the quality of information around us, and we can move from high-quality research to a random website, hardly noticing the switch. Today more than ever the confidence to be 'critical' about any and everything is probably *the* most important take-way gain you will make in the course of your studies.

In researching this section I googled 'evaluating web sources'.[4] I looked at 20 or 30 different sites and chased links all over the world. I travelled many continents: North America, the UK, Australasia, Asia. I visited some of the major universities in the world, found a great site for seven-year-olds, and some homespun advice from individuals. But for my present purpose?

---

4 For suggestions for other guides see 'Useful sources'.

A critical look at the URL

As with a reading list, it helps to have an idea about an item before you go there. Look at the URL (the address) for clues. It gives an indication (but no more, since anyone can set up a company and country codes can be misleading) about the nature of the site.

While your fingers are tapping, get your brain thinking – critically! Your critical approach to web sources starts **before you leave the results page!**

The main part of the web address: company or organisation

a non-profit organisation

country where the organisation actually is.

http://www.nice.org.uk/

What to expect	In the URL
Commercial organisation or company, big or small	.com (US or anywhere) or .co.uk (UK)
The country where the outfit is: France, Australia, UK, South Africa etc.	.fr .au .uk .sa etc.
A non-profit organisation	.org
Academic institutions	.edu (US) .ac.uk (UK)
A government agency	.gov

Then start your critical scanning before reading. Give yourself a framework by using a set of evaluation criteria – here the 'strategic questions'.

The strategic questions – again!

And overarching all these specific questions is the big one:
So what …?

So what … are the implications for other research in this area? … for future practice? Will I use this material in my assignment? How?

What … is being said?

Why … is it there?

Any website or reading

How … good is it to use?

When … does the info date from?

Where … is the organisation/person located?

Who … has produced the site?

Will I use this material in my assignment? How?

So… what are the implications of this?

What is being said?	**So what?** ... are the implications?

- ▸ Fact? How do you know it's correct? Opinion? Whose? Argument? Based on what evidence?
- ▸ What evidence is there for statements/data?
- ▸ Does it show the sources of statements/data? References? Useful links?
- ▸ Is it the right level of detail for your purpose?
- ▸ Does the information here match with what you know already?
- ▸ Check it against a completely different source.

Why is it there?	**So what?** ... are the implications?

- ▸ What is the purpose or aim of the site? See 'About us' or similar.
- ▸ Why did they put this material up? To give access to information? Explain? Persuade? Sell?

Who has produced the site?	**So what?** ... are the implications?

- ▸ An individual? An organisation? Who are they? Can you contact them?
- ▸ How are they qualified to produce this material?
- ▸ Do they produce material in other formats – reports, books?
- ▸ Do other sources (like journals) use it?
- ▸ What sites does it link to?

But is it any good? Evaluating (web) sources 35

How good is it to use?	**So what?** … are the implications?

- User friendly? Starts from the perspective of a new user, not the webmaster?
- Logical, easy to navigate?

When does this information date from?	**So what?** … are the implications?

- Does the material/data and its sources have dates?
- When was it last updated (see bottom of page)? If there is a date, use it for your reference.
- Is it kept maintained? Do the links work?

Where are they from?	**So what?** … are the implications?

- Do they have a real address and telephone number? Check 'About us/Contact us'.

9 A critical record of reading: an annotated bibliography

Students may be set the task of showing their 'critical' approach to their reading in an 'annotated bibliography'.

What is an 'annotated bibliography'?

A 'bibliography' in this context means the sources – books, articles, reports, websites, databases etc. – that you have read or consulted. It is in effect your research footprints, the trail you have taken to the point where you start writing your assignment. 'Annotations' are notes you make on each source, in which you record brief comments about it, and its relevance to you. It will normally be short: three sentences or so.

Why do an annotated bibliography?

It encourages you to think critically about what you have read in preparation for writing. It also helps your reader to select their reading (useful in group tasks), and of course it makes your research footprints explicit to your tutor/reader. It is often used as a midpoint in a bigger assignment.

A short annotation: what do I include?

Read your guidance carefully! It will probably tell you what to include and give you an indication of length. In 100–150 words you can probably achieve the following:

The full reference (not included in word count)	
Summary What is it about?	• The author's purpose, aim or question. • Main argument, central idea, findings or conclusions. • What sort of text is it? General? Specific?
Evaluation What do I think about it?	• Who is it written for? • Particular strengths, from your point of view. • Any weaknesses or limitations?
Reflection How might I use it?	Has the text helped you understanding something better? How useful is it? Will you use it? How?

In a short annotation, the three elements will probably be of approximately equal length. Don't overrun on the summary and slip into describing the text – there are no Brownie points for that! It is your reactions and reflections that count. That 'critical' thing …

An example

Regina is researching an essay on the recruitment and retention of healthcare professionals in the NHS. Below is one annotation from her annotated bibliography.

Mills EJ, Schabas WA, Volmink J, Walker R, Ford N, Katabina E, Anema A, Joffres M, Cahn P and Montaner J (2008). Should active recruitment of health workers from sub-Saharan Africa be viewed as a crime? *The Lancet.* 371, Feb. 23, pp. 685–88.

Powerful argument – that wealthy countries contribute directly to worsening healthcare in poor sub-Saharan African countries, by actively recruiting h/c staff (doctors, nurses, pharmacists). Uses country-by-country WHO stats. Argues that it is unethical and contravenes various legal agreements.

Very readable, clearly and logically written, relevant to anyone interested in the negative impact of wealthy countries on poor countries today. Persuasive detail and good refs to wide range of sources (specific studies, international bodies, government and legal sources).

I was really shocked by the article, and hadn't been aware of this aspect of employing healthcare workers from other countries. May make this the focus of my essay, and need to research further.

You may even come to welcome having to write annotations! It gets you into the habit of standing back from what you have read, looking down on it and capturing what you thought of it. This is something you will develop the habit of doing anyway, as you become a more thoughtful – yes, critical – and confident student, leaving the sponge model of learning behind you.

As you find you know more, and understand better, ideas begin to take shape in your mind. If you look back to the 'stairway' on p. 12, you are now at the 'synthesis' point, when things start to come together.

You are ready to start planning your writing.

What does it say?
How are they different?
How do I use it?

GETTING CRITICAL IN WRITING

That point when you have completed the bulk of your reading and before you start writing is indeed 'critical'. It's essential – mission-critical – and it is the point at which you gain control of what you have read. You review your reading and notes, and start to work with it. It comes together as a synthesis.

It is 'synthesis with a purpose' because you have to use it in a particular way. You have to use it to 'answer' the question you have been set. The question is there to help you think critically, to stop you writing pages of all-I-know-about, to guide you in focusing and selecting, to draw your attention to conflicts of evidence, interpretation and argument in the topic area. It is your invitation to join the discussion. So …

10 Answer the question!

Look back to your strategic reading of your course handbook (p. 2–3) and double-check that you have all the guidance you need to be crystal clear about what you have to do. Comments on returned work like:

'So what does all this tell us about the question?'

'Why are you telling us about this?'

suggest that previously you have not kept the task in sharp focus throughout. This matters because a key way of showing your critical approach in your writing is by selecting only the materials and discussion that relate directly to the 'question' you have been asked.

But what if there isn't a question as such? If you were given a statement to write about, or a broad topic to explore, how do you show your critical approach?

Look again. There is always a question in your title. It may be **explicit** (with a question mark) or it may be **implicit** in the instruction, or **hidden** in a bald title. You have to spot it, dig for it or create it. And then address it from start to finish.

Critical analysis in your writing starts here.

Getting critical with your 'question'

The explicit question

How far …? *How convincing is …?* *How successful …?* *Do you agree that …?* *In what ways …?* *What is the role of …?* *Can …?* ***To what extent …?***	**The challenge here** is to pick the question apart, ask questions about it, and plan how to answer it. You show your critical approach by developing an argument, linking each point to one or other aspect of the question, and reaching a conclusion. The answer will usually be on a spectrum between 'Not at all' and 'yes totally'. If it were one of these extremes there would be little point in asking the question!

The instruction 'question'

Analyse the … *Compare and contrast the approaches to …* *Consider the impact of …* ***Discuss and evaluate** …*	**The challenge here** is to appreciate what the 'instruction' word is asking for, and show your critical understanding of the topic by picking your way through the complexities. You show your critical awareness by doing exactly what it says!

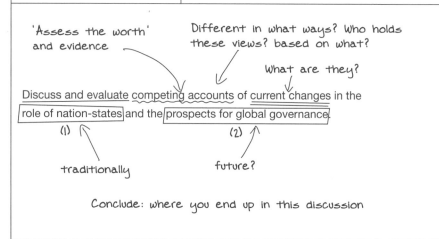

'Assess the worth' and evidence

Different in what ways? Who holds these views? based on what?

What are they?

<u>Discuss and evaluate</u> <u>competing</u> accounts of <u>current</u> changes in the

| role of nation-states | and the | prospects for global governance |

(1)

traditionally

(2)

future?

Conclude: where you end up in this discussion

The bald title 'question'

Future developments in the airline sector	**The challenge here** is to create a structure for your essay by pulling out the headings hidden within the broad topic title, and picking out the debates within these specific areas. Show your critical understanding of these debates.
The equality and difference debate	
Going green: introducing an environmental management plan in the hotel industry	

The Early Years Leader and change

This glimpse of some of the things you might be asked to do in an essay or assignment is to show how you are always being asked to 'answer' a 'question',[5] however it is phrased. You are never being asked to write-all-you-know-about. The 'critical' dimension runs throughout: in the skill in pinpointing the question, unpacking the question(s), setting the question yourself, and capturing the debates or complications in the topic. Finding your sense of direction or purpose through it all from start to finish is where your 'argument' lies. This is key to critical writing.

---

5 For more on how to analyse essay and assignment questions and plan your answer, see *Planning Your Essay* in this series.

Writing paragraphs: a critical skill

Written work is divided into paragraphs. Mastering this basic unit of writing will give you the vehicle for showing your critical skills. The paragraph is in effect the unit of argument – each one is an interlocking link in your essay, leading to a conclusion.

Here's why ... paragraphs are important

Paragraphs have a structure:

▶ A paragraph develops **one main idea**.

▶ This main idea is usually expressed clearly in one sentence, the first, or **'topic sentence'**.

▶ Paragraphs have a beginning, a middle and an end. The sentences in the middle explain, develop, illustrate or modify the main idea in the topic sentence. The last sentence often returns to the idea in the topic sentence to show how it has developed.

Paragraph structure has a purpose. It makes it easier to:

▶ **Read:** the main idea is first, and you know that this idea will be developed before you move on.

▶ **Plan:** each paragraph develops a single point. You can plan by mapping out the points.

▶ **Write:** new point, new paragraph. Start each paragraph with a clear statement of the point you are making, then add detail.

Here's how ... to write a paragraph

All you need to write a paragraph is an idea of what you want to say, a point you want to put across. A paragraph is how you develop this idea into a short block of text, and your essay builds up paragraph by paragraph.

A paragraph plan

1 **Start with the topic sentence** to express the main idea.
2 **Explain or define any abstract, key or problematic terms** to clarify the topic sentence.
3 **Show your evidence** to support your main idea or argument in the topic sentence.
4 **Comment on the evidence** to show how it supports or develops the main idea. If appropriate, mention other evidence (examples/studies/experiments/interpretations) to widen the discussion.
5 **Conclude**. Look back to your topic sentence and ask yourself:
   ▸ how have I moved on/developed the main idea in it?
   ▸ where am I going next?
   ▸ Then write the last sentence.

Source: Williams (1995, pp. 45–47;1996, pp. 34–44). Many of the approaches and ideas in this guide – this section in particular – have developed from earlier publications on study skills.

Activity

Below is a paragraph from a student's essay. How does it match the paragraph plan? Try adding the numbers of the paragraph plan above to the text.

The Early Years Leader (EYL) needs to have an understanding of how teams work if they are to be effective in managing staff groups and change. An effective team will most likely go through stages of development (Hartley 1997). These stages have been described by Tuckman and Jensen (1977) as 'Forming' (a group gets to know each other), 'Storming' (some initial conflict develops), 'Norming' (group norms are established), 'Performing' (the group communicates and collaborates well) and 'Adjourning' (the group disbands). This cycle is repeated when new objectives are adopted or there is a change in team members, but to be able to perform to its optimum, a team needs to go through these stages to reach the 'performing' stage. It is the role of the Early Years Leader (EYL) to move the team through these stages trying to balance individual, professional and organisational needs and development.

1 The Early Years Leader (EYL) needs to have an understanding of how teams work if they are to be effective in managing staff groups and change. **2** An effective team will most likely go through stages of development (Hartley 1997). **3** These stages have been described by Tuckman and Jensen (1977) as 'Forming' (a group gets to know each other), 'Storming' (some initial conflict develops), 'Norming' (group norms are established), 'Performing' (the group communicates and collaborates well) and 'Adjourning' (the group disbands). **4** This cycle is repeated when new objectives are adopted or there is a change in team members, but to be able to perform to its optimum, a team needs to go through these stages to reach the 'performing' stage. **4** It is the role of the Early Years Leader (EYL) to move **5** the team through these stages trying to balance individual, professional and organisational needs and development.

1. Topic sentence

2. Explain/define

3. Show your evidence

4. Comment

4. Comment

5. Conclude

DIY paragraph checking

Try checking the paragraph plan against:

▶ a paragraph of something you are reading;
▶ a paragraph you are writing.

Don't expect it to tally exactly, but you should be able to see a structure, with the topic sentence clearly stated at the beginning and elements of the 'plan' in the rest of the paragraph – even if it is just one or two words.

The paragraph plan and critical thinking

What happens when paragraphs don't follow this plan?

The *So what?* problem

You have main point, topic sentence (1), explanation (2), illustration, explanation, evidence (3):

> **1** The Early Years Leader (EYL) needs to have an understanding of how teams work if they are to be effective in managing staff groups and change. **2** An effective team will most likely go through stages of development (Hartley 1997). **3** These stages have been described by Tuckman and Jensen (1977) as 'Forming' (a group gets to know each other), 'Storming' (some initial conflict develops), 'Norming' (group norms are established), 'Performing' (the group communicates and collaborates well) and 'Adjourning' (the group disbands).

1. Topic sentence (main point)

2. Explanation

3. Illustration, explanation, evidence

But then you stop and move on to the next point in a new paragraph:

> The Early Years Foundation Stage places a great deal of emphasis on …

No Number 4. No comment from you, no evaluation, no evidence to the reader that you have understood what you have set out, no indication of how this evidence relates to the point you are making – and therefore no argument. The reader is left thinking '*So…?*' Or '*But what does this tell us about …?*' or even '**So what?**'

The remedy

Make sure you have a Number 4: a comment on your 'evidence', however short.
In the example above the Number 4 comment peeps through in several phrases:

This writer …
evaluates the usefulness of these
ideas, picks out key aspects

> **4**This cycle is repeated when new objectives are adopted or there is a change
> in team members, but to be able to perform to its optimum, a team needs to
> go through these stages to reach the 'performing' stage. **4**It is the role of the
> Early Years Leader (EYL) to move the team through these stages trying to
> **5**balance individual, professional and organisational needs and development.

and links it back to
the topic sentence

applies the theory to
the situation

Other ways of showing you have a perspective on the material you discuss include:

- highlighting the differences between two studies
- showing you understand the points made, or the weight of argument, eg, 'key to
  this is …' 'It seems that …'
- connecting with the issues implicit in the question.

These are a few of the ways of showing that you are on top of the material you have read and are able to move around it, talking to your reader about the sense *you* make of it. In short, in your Number 4 you show your critical awareness of what you are writing about.

> **Key point**: Answer the 'So what?' question before your reader has time to ask it! Make your comments.

How long is a paragraph?

How long is a piece of string? Long enough to do what you want it to? Or not? The same applies to paragraphs. A paragraph needs to be long enough to develop a point or idea in the way outlined in the paragraph plan.

For the academic writing of most students 5–8 sentences is a good guideline. Are you within this range? Try the upside down test.

The upside down test

Turn your essay or assignment upside down and turn the pages. Does it look inviting to read?

This big block of text is most off-putting. It also tells your reader that you have not structured your argument into separate points, and you blur everything together.

The remedy? Read through carefully, spotting when you move onto a new point, and make this a new paragraph. Check you have clear topic sentences.

This is off-putting too. Your reader will assume that you have a 'shopping list' approach to points and ideas. You can't develop a point properly in one or two sentences.

The remedy? It may be that some of your mini-bites belong together. Run them together to form a paragraph. Or it may be that you have lots of points, each a topic sentence in itself. Try using the paragraph plan to develop each point.

58 **GETTING CRITICAL**

Satisfying customers should be the overriding aim of marketing activity. To what extent does the literature?

This definition covers the important point that the needs and objectives of both the customer and the organisation must be satisfied. Satisfying customers should be an essential part of marketing activity for it is cheaper to satisfy and thereby retain existing customers than it is to obtain new ones (Oliver 1999). According to Masterson et al (2006) it costs approximately five times more to attract new customers that it does to keep an existing customers happy. Conversely it needs to be considered that even within a customer base not all patrons will be profitable to the company. In retail banking for example, the This definition covers the important point that the needs and objectives of both the customer and the organisation

Must be satisfied. Satisfying customers should be an essential part of marketing activity for it is cheaper to satisfy and thereby retain existing customers than it is to obtain new ones (Oliver 1999). According to Masterson et al (2006) it costs approximately five times more to attract new customers that it does to keep an existing customer happy. Conversely it needs to be considered that even within a customer base not all patrons will be profitable to the company. In retail banking for example, the This definition covers the important point that the needs and objectives of both the customer and the organisation must be satisfied. Satisfying customers should be an essential part of marketing activity for it is cheaper to satisfy and thereby retain existing customers than it is to obtain new ones (Oliver 1999). According to Masterson et al (2006) it costs approximately

Five times more to attract new customers that it does to keep an existing customer happy. Conversely it needs to be considered that even within a customer base not all patrons will be profitable to the company. In retail banking for example, the This definition covers the important point that the needs and objectives of both the customer and the organisation must be satisfied. Satisfying customers should be an essential part of marketing activity for it is cheaper to satisfy and thereby retain existing customers than it is to obtain new ones (Oliver 1999). According to Masterson et al (2006) it costs approximately five times more to attract new customers that it does to keep an existing customer happy. Conversely it needs to be considered that even within a customer base not all patrons will be profitable to the company.

This definition covers the important point that the needs and objectives of both the customer and the organisation must be satisfied. Satisfying customers should be an essential part of marketing activity for it is cheaper to satisfy and thereby retain existing customers than it is to obtain new. it does to keep an existing customer happy. Conversely it needs to be considered that even within a customer.

A page of writing should look something like this – this time the right way up, with paragraphs moving down the page looking like they are long enough to develop an idea, but not so long that they merge ideas or ramble.

This is very rough and ready – allow for differences in line spacing, variation between different sections of your essay, the norms in different subject areas – but use these images as a jog to check your paragraphing. This is an essential tool in demonstrating your ability to see key points and to set out a coherent argument or account. These qualities are fundamental to critical thinking, analysis and writing.

12 The 'critical' bit in essays and assignments

This section takes a closer look at what that 'critical' dimension can look like on the page.

'Tell me more …'

First, let's take a look at statements that leave a reader thinking something like: 'Where are you in all this? Where is your voice, your comment, your understanding of why it matters? Tell me more …'

Below are extracts from the first draft of essays and assignments by several students. The comments on the right are the sort a critical but friendly reader might make to help these writers to develop their own 'voice' and show their critical awareness of what they are writing. They can then use this feedback to produce their final draft.

| 1 | Letbridge (1997) argues that communication skills support and pervade the whole concept of working in partnership. Moreover, professionals are less effective on their service users' behalf if they cannot communicate precisely and persuasively (Lodge 2000). Stanley (2003) comments that to …◄ | *For your redraft*: Take a deep breath and talk to your reader. Explain the implications of these observations for work with clients.

A critical thinker will **apply** their reading to their situation, not just describe it. | *A tutor might think 'So ...??' I can see you have read widely and summarise key points well, but where are you going with it? Tell us why this matters.* |
| 2 | Even though women have a guaranteed job, after maternity leave they often find themselves competing against their replacement on their return. | *For your redraft*: Check you have good evidence for this comment. If not, take it out – it may not be essential to your wider argument.

A critical thinker will make sure their statements are based on **evidence** the reader can check. | *A tutor may write 'Evidence??' in the margin. I'd like to know how you know this. Common sense? Personal experience? Neither of these are the sorts of evidence you need to support an assertion like this.* |

| 3 | Men are often considered to be more computer literate, which enables them to understand and do things at a faster rate than women (Donoghue 2007). | *For your redraft*: Think hard about whether this is a point that helps your overall argument. If you still want to make it, do more extensive research to satisfy yourself as to whether there is good evidence for your statement.

A critical thinker will **ask questions** about the quality of their sources, and not use material with weak evidence. | *Tutor comment: 'Not a credible source'.* Every reader will want to check your source for this (contentious) statement! Your reference shows that it was 'Travel Weekly', which is not a reliable source for a statement like this! It won't be based on high quality research. |
| 4 | Bowlby's theory of attachment showed that 'the infant and young child should experience a warm, intimate and continuous relationship with his mother or mother substitute ...' (1982 p11). Rutter (1981) also found 'the child is more likely to develop deviant behaviour' (p18) ... | *For your redraft*: Explain the differences between the theories of these two writers, in your own words – 'Number 4' in the paragraph plan. Too many quotes makes your writing disjointed. Cut down on the quotes drastically.
A critical thinker will only **quote** key, special words, and then **comment** making sure their own voice comes through. | A tutor might think: you hop from quote to quote. Don't be nervous about summarising and commenting on these theories. Your voice, your interpretation is missing. Go for it! Have you got a Number 4 somewhere? |

A few take-away points

To become a critical thinker (and so a writer), be prepared to challenge yourself. Come back to your first draft after a break (ideally of several days), and you will be better able to see it with fresh eyes.

As a critical reader of your own writing, try to:

▶ **Ask questions:** you could start with the strategic questions, and adapt them.
▶ Look for **evidence** for statements or assertions.
▶ Check for **assumptions and personal views** with no wider basis in evidence.
▶ Check for sweeping statements and **generalisations** – a comment that may be true of one situation but not true when applied to others.
▶ Probe the **knowledge** base of the writing – superficial or in-depth? Do you really understand it? (If you don't as a writer, your reader certainly won't!)
▶ Find your **voice** as a writer. *Tell me why it matters or how it is different. Explain the implications, applications, uses. Talk to me, your reader.*

Know what you're aiming at

It figures that in order to write critically, you need to know what you are aiming at and, for this, models are helpful. Ideally, tutors will run this as an exercise – discussing past essays that got a range of marks, so you can see and understand the differences that lead to different gradings. You can, however, do this yourself.

Use any feedback you have. Look back at marked essays, working out why you got each tick, and what each comment means. If you look at a few essays you will probably see a pattern emerging – what needs to be on your personal hit list? If you can do this with other students, all taking the approach 'we need to understand the feedback' (not be negative, or personal), you could all learn a lot.

Using feedback

Below is, first, some tutor feedback on 'A' grade essays and assignments, including some from the 'critical soup' on p. 7 . Hopefully the 'soup' will become clearer as you look through the following pages. Then come extracts from 'A' grade essays and assignments. Some of the comments really do relate to the extracts, some to other 'A' grade work. See if you can work out which is which!

Tutor feedback on 'A' grade work

You have considered several issues arising from the relevant literature and you have explained and analysed them …
Good discussion of theoretical concepts. Excellent use of supporting evidence to illustrate arguments.
Well referenced, using articles from the reading list plus other relevant sources including relevant peer-reviewed articles.
Argument is succinctly and unequivocally stated in the introduction.
This essay shows a high level of knowledge and understanding of the debates and advances a coherent and convincing argument.
You have identified all the relevant debates and theories surrounding this subject. Your critical analysis is of a high standard …
You have read extensively and use the empirical evidence that you have found to support your arguments, and in your analysis …

Extract from 'A' grade student essays and assignments

A	Although empowerment is a management initiative, this does not necessarily mean that empowerment is not of benefit to employees. Hertzberg's two-factor theory of motivation at work (Hertzberg et al 1959 cited in Mullins 1998) clearly shows that responsibility and recognition are motivators that lead to job satisfaction. The problem is that not all employees can be categorised under Herzberg's framework. Many employees only work to earn money. Argyris (1998) label these as 'externally committed' (p89). When trying to empower staff, these are the people that …	*A thoughtful, critical comment in the topic sentence, direct from the writer* *This short summary from a key source shows the writer has understood, and selected only the key point needed for their discussion.* *A 'Number 4' comment! The writer's own comment, identifying the limitations of this theory, and moving swiftly to explore the theory of another author.* *Good 'synthesis' (see p13) linking ideas and theories in a discussion*
B	There is considerable consensus about the impact of early experience, although there have been some dissenting voices. These include Harris (1998) who questioned the extent of parental influence, and considered the influence of peers to be greater. This, however, is unlikely to be the case in the first few years of life. Kagan (1998) has been a strong opponent of the notion of 'infant determinism' (p62), and …	*A clear topic sentence, making the writer's point for the paragraph, and indicating wide reading in order to be able to say this – with authority.* *A short, sharp summary showing the writer's understanding of these authors.* *A 'Number 4' comment! The writer has reflected on the theory and made a brief comment of their own before moving on to the next theorist. In contrast see (1) on p62*

| C | … In this essay I argue that it is not possible to solve global environmental problems within the structure of the global political economy because the principles which underpin the competitive free market unavoidably exploit the environment. However … it is important to consider what intervention in the global economy might involve, and what it might achieve. | *To set out an argument so clearly in the introduction, the writer must have read and thought a lot before they begin. Issues are never black or white. This writer will pick their way carefully discussing conflicting evidence to show what they conclude and why.*

The writer uses language carefully and critically. Not 'solve' but it might 'achieve' something. |

Look back, move forward!

Before you leave this section, look back to the introduction to this book (p. vii):
You need to be more critical …

Now flick through the pages you have read … hopefully you will feel that you have been on a journey, one that has taken you to where you need to be as a critical, questioning and confident student.

This may be where you leave this book. Now just do it! And enjoy.

Another time, you may want to look at Part 4, 'Critical steps'. It takes a closer look at:

- the critical steps outlined in Part 1 (in the 'stairway'); and
- using a 'framework' as part of your critical analysis.

PART
4 CRITICAL STEPS

This section is for dipping into. Chapter 13 takes a closer look at each step in the 'stairway' to critical thinking (see p. 13) from bottom to top – starting with the addition of 'Describe'.

Chapter 14 considers how to use a framework as a 'tool' to help with critical analysis.

Stepping up the stairway to critical thinking

Describe

DESCRIBE	Understand	Comprehend the key points, assumptions, arguments and evidence presented.
Process		Take in the information, i.e. what you have read, heard, seen or done.

Students often worry that their work is 'descriptive' not 'analytical', and tutors' comments often underline this. To be able to 'describe' is an essential first step. As the 'stairway' suggests, you need to take in (or 'process') information, and make sure you understand it. Describing is, however, only a first step and at university you are usually expected to go beyond this.

But how do I know I'm describing?

If you feel you have to keep going to tell the story (an account, case study, observation), panicking because you've written four pages and only just got to … and there is so much more … up hill and down dale …

… then you are describing: *what this and that writer said/practitioner did/you observed.*

The remedy?

STOP!
Step back! Get a perspective …
Step up to analysis.

Analyse

Analysis is defined as: 'the resolution of anything complex into its simple elements' (*Shorter Oxford English Dictionary*, 1983).

Analysis is the foundation to critical thinking. Its lowly place in the stairway underplays its crucial importance. In reality it is the foundation of critical thinking, because if you can't see the 'key components' and how they 'fit together' (Open University 2008), you can't manipulate them, think about them, work out their merits or use them.

	Analyse	Examine how these key components fit together and relate to each other.

Stop the narrative, stop telling the story, look down on the situation, see the themes. Pick out key points that illustrate the themes. Relate them to lecture or course topics. And stick to the word count.

Compare (and contrast)

	Compare	Explore the similarities and differences between the ideas you are reading about.

If you are asked to 'compare' you will also 'contrast'. In things that are very different, the similarities are interesting. In things that are very similar, the differences are more interesting. So inevitably you do both (to a greater or lesser extent) when you are asked to do either.

Synthesise

Bring together different sources of information to serve an argument or idea you are constructing. Make logical connections between the different sources that help you shape and support your ideas.	Synthesise

This is another powerhouse process. It's what you do when you put together your thoughts, along with your reading and notes, when it all comes together for you – click! Often you need to start writing to make this happen. Just remember that what you are writing is a draft and you may need to bin it!

Evaluate

Assess the worth of an idea in terms of its relevance to your needs, the evidence on which it is based and how it relates to other pertinent ideas.	**Evaluate**	

You've thought about the relationship between ideas and interpretations; now you look more carefully at each one to consider its merits, the evidence or argument on which it is based. You consider its 'valu' to your situation or problem, where it might be useful, what its limitations are.

EVALUATE

Apply

Transfer the understanding you have gained from your critical evaluation and use in response to questions, assignments and projects.	**Apply**	

We are now getting towards the top of the staircase. The great buzz with learning comes when you find that ideas can transform the way you see things. On the surface perhaps nothing has changed, but you know you see things differently. You understand. You have become someone who can use – or reject or refute – ideas or approaches in your own work, whether this is a further exploration of ideas, or whether there is a more direct application for your insights as a practitioner.

Adapted from Godwin (2009)

Justify

Use critical thinking to develop arguments, draw conclusions, make inferences and identify implications.	Justify

This is where you stand up and are counted. You are able to say not only what you did or thought but *why* you did it or thought it. You are able to argue, defend, justify. Your essay will have the **golden thread of argument**, running from start to finish, from introduction to conclusion. Better still, you may end with the 'What if? What next?' questions – the implications.

Thinking up models to explain and interpret the world around us – or at least that bit we are engaged in studying – is a fundamental analytical response to being alive and thinking. There are a few models in this guide already:

▶ the 'stairway' to critical thinking (of course!) (pp.12, 69),
▶ the research comfort zone triangle (p. 25),
▶ the mention of the dynamic of group processes (p. 52).

'Model' and 'framework' are both terms for thinking structures that people have developed to help critical analysis. If you are asked to use a 'framework' in an analysis, what is it you are being asked to do?

About frameworks

Whatever issues you are considering, you are not the first person ever to do so. You are building on work that has gone before, by other people who have been there before. These researchers have not necessarily had exactly the same experiences or thoughts in exactly the same contexts, but they have been in similar situations, researched and reflected on them, and developed a way of categorising characteristics, or looking at a situation that may be helpful to other people – you, for example.

Using a framework can help you:

▶ see different aspects or elements more clearly – easy to lose in the muddle of reality or the whirl of ideas or conflicting approaches. This is 'analysis'.
▶ pick out key themes or aspects, and stop you telling the story of what you did, read or thought. This avoids 'description'.
▶ make changes in what you do: to step up from anecdote and adopt a more systematic or better justified basis for actions. This is 'application'.

Frameworks can help you to think critically, by giving you some fixed points for doing your basic analysis, on which you can then build your own interpretations, reflections and applications.

See the difference when you add a picture frame to a sketch! It goes from being just something that's happening to something you stand back and look at and reflect on.

This section illustrates this with a brief look at a few well-used frameworks.

Using a framework for analysis: SWOT

This model is most often used in business-related subjects, but it is also used in a wide range of contexts: for example, by a GP practice on a training day, or by people considering career options.

Here you are asked to consider the internal **S**trengths and **W**eaknesses of an organisation (usually), and the **O**pportunities and **T**hreats it faces externally (hence SWOT).

Internal factors **Looking** *in* (to yourself, an organisation) what are your/their …	External factors **Looking** *out* (to the external environment in which you or the organisation is operating) what are the …
STRENGTHS	OPPORTUNITIES
WEAKNESSES	THREATS

Only after you have completed the analysis do you consider what you DO next, with a critical discussion of the options, hopefully leading to an action plan (for yourself or to recommend to an organisation).

Try it!

On yourself: considering a career move.

Looking *in*	Looking *out*
STRENGTHS What are you good at? What do you enjoy? **WEAKNESSES** What do you struggle with?	**OPPORTUNITIES** What's out there that could use what you're good at? And your enthusiasm? **THREATS** What could limit you? Developments on the horizon that make it more difficult?

An analysis using fixed points like these SWOT analyses helps you distance yourself from the 'story' or case study, and become analytical. You pick out key points and allocate them to different headings in a systematic way. As a 'tool' it will usually go in the appendix. So what goes in your text? Your critical discussion informed by your reading and other sources of ideas as you compare, contrast, evaluate, justify – or do whatever you have been asked to on the basis of this underpinning analysis.

On an organisation. Typical general questions are shown first. Key points from a student's SWOT analysis of a restaurant is shown in small bullet points.

Looking *in*	Looking *out*
STRENGTHS What are they successful at? Do well? ▸ Good local reputation ▸ Good location (wealthy village and on high street) ▸ Fairly well trained staff and low turnover ▸ Locally sourced food	**OPPORTUNITIES** How could they use their strengths to achieve something extra? ▸ Closure of L'Orangerie restaurant in March ▸ Growing customer interest in local food ▸ Trend away from brands
WEAKNESSES What lets them down, or risks letting them down in terms of (for example) staff or systems or purpose? ▸ Limited parking ▸ Old property (small kitchen) ▸ No online booking ▸ Little promotion	**THREATS** What external factors or developments could impact negatively? ▸ Credit crunch/recession – esp on classier dining out ▸ Opening of Piazza brasserie in June ▸ Dependent on access by car and petrol costs

Combining frameworks

You can use two or more models or frameworks to analyse a situation, in a complementary way. Here is an example.

Group development and team roles

Students are sometimes asked to write a 'reflective account' or a 'critical reflection' on the process of their group in working towards the eventual product – a poster, report or whatever. Here it is very easy to become descriptive, telling the story of the process: *x did this, y said that, we all thought* … etc. This is not what is required.

You are being asked to relate your experience of the pleasures and pitfalls of working in a group to the research, thinking and reflection of others who have been there before – just as with any other 'framework'. The challenge is to relate theory to practice, which can feel difficult when what you are doing seems so everyday and routine. This is where a framework is useful. Try this approach as a starting point.

First, analyse the overall progress of your group towards the end product, using the framework mentioned in the paragraph on p. 52. Use the headings for your analysis.

Framework 1: Stages of group development

Forming	A group of people gets together, by choice or allocation.
Storming	Differences of view or approach emerge and conflict arises.
Norming	The group sets to work, and takes on roles and tasks.
Performing	The group works well and delivers.
Adjourning	The group completes its task and disbands.

Source: Boddy (2008, pp. 570–72). This text is one of many that discuss and develop the original model by Tuckman and Jensen (1977).

Not that it will feel like this! And not all groups get through all the stages. Whatever the outcome, it is your task to analyse what is going on, for better or worse. To what extent was it similar to the process outlined in this model? And in what ways was it different? An account that develops from this sort of analysis, comparing the theory with the practice, will have a critical dimension.

You could combine this consideration of the overall process of the group with an analysis of the roles of each individual.

Framework 2: Team roles

Many thinkers have analysed the working of teams or groups in terms of the role or roles each individual takes on and how they interact. Belbin (1993) researched team interactions and came up with this model.

Belbin's nine team roles:

1	**Plant:** creative, imaginative, unorthodox	6	**Teamworker:** cooperative, mild, perceptive and diplomatic
2	**Resource investigator:** extrovert, enthusiastic, communicative	7	**Implementer:** disciplined, reliable, conservative, efficient
3	**Coordinator:** mature, confident, a good chairperson	8	**Completer:** painstaking, conscientious, anxious
4	**Shaper:** challenging, dynamic, thrives on pressure	9	**Specialist:** single-minded, self-starting, dedicated
5	**Monitor–evaluator:** sober, strategic, discerning		

Source: Belbin (1993). This short extract only gives the role name and description of characteristics.

You can use the profiles as a starting point for analysing the roles of your actual team members, and write a critical account of how they interact in the course of carrying out the task set. In a group of, say, four people, each person will combine roles, and they may well overlap and change. Again, it lifts you out of any temptation to tell the story of the group, and offers a basis for analysis and critical thinking.

Developing frameworks

Frameworks develop. They are organic, part of the intellectual process on which research is based. Researchers are often described as 'standing on the shoulders of giants', with new discoveries and developments and ways of thinking building on what went before. This is the core business of research and critical thinking.

You may find yourself feeling that the framework you are using does not quite work for you. Clearly Boddy (2008) did. He discusses both the frameworks outlined above and develops and amends them. He also gives the reference to the original work so the reader can track the original framework and use it if they prefer – which I did with Belbin.

Here are some more examples:

The 'Stairway to critical thinking' (Open University 2008)	I have developed this in this guide to show the text as a staircase, with one process building on the next.
Group development (Tuckman and Jensen 1977)	Maureen Guirdham (2002) has developed this to show how the focus on individual, group and task needs changes through the stages. Interesting.
A SWOT analysis is often combined with a PEST analysis in business (Political, Economic, Social, Technical) in analysing the opportunities and threats in the external environment …	… to which a final E – for 'Ecological' – has been added in recent years to reflect the growing importance of this aspect.

… and so on.

Getting critical with a framework

If you decide to amend an existing framework, you are in good company, part of the mainstream of academic evolution. It will be the outcome of some hard critical thinking. You have to justify the changes you want to make, showing the strengths of the particular framework and its uses, but also its limitations as a tool for the analysis you want to make. Part of your justification will come from other things you have read, and you will need to show the basis for the changes you want to make in the same way as you need to show the evidence for any other point or argument.

You can, of course, develop your own framework … and if you decide to do this you are flying beyond the scope of this guide! Enjoy!

15 Becoming a writer

So what is that critical thing? I hope you can now see that the critical dimension is a mindset you bring to your work. You can do it once you have the confidence to take control of your studies. It is a bit like turning a little chunk of rock in the sun and suddenly seeing the light catch a sparkle.

There is nothing magical about it, but you do have to work at it. At no point does good work just happen. It is the outcome of reading, analysis, reflection, asking questions, and then recording the outcomes of this process in *your* writing. It is hard work.

Writing is a craft: if you work at it, you will get better at it. When you start to rewrite your work because you want it to be better, you know you are a writer – and a critical one at that. When you are a writer, your 'voice' will come through. It is your analysis, reflection and interpretation so of course you the author will show through, making sense to your reader. Let's hope your reader in turn will feel moved to write:

> '*You have engaged with the debates in the subject and your critical analysis is of a high standard ...*'

Go for it!

Timeline: planning the term or semester

Wk	Module	Module	Module	Module
1				
2				
3				
4				
5				
6				
7				
8				
9				
10				
11				
12				

and then ... exams?

| 13 | | | | |

References

Belbin M (1993). *Team roles at work.* Oxford: Elsevier Butterworth Heinemann.

Boddy D (2008). *Management: an introduction*, 4th edition. Harlow: Pearson.

Godwin J (2009). *Planning your essay*. Basingstoke: Palgrave Macmillan.

Guirdham M (2002). *Interactive behaviour at work*, 3rd edition. Harlow: Pearson.

Open University (2008). *Critical thinking.* Available at: http://www.opwn.ac.uk/skillsforstudy/critical-thinking.php [Accessed 26 October 2008].

Osborne T and Kiker C (2005). Carbon offsets as an economic alternative to large-scale logging: a case study in Guyama. *Ecological Economics* Volume 52, Issue 4 (1 March), pp481–96. Elsevier ScienceDirect.

Shorter Oxford English Dictionary (1983). 3rd edition. Oxford: Oxford University Press.

Tuckman BW and Jensen MA (1977). Stages in small group development revisited. *Group and Organisation Studies* 2, pp419–27.

Williams K (1995). *Writing essays.* Developing writing series. Oxford: Oxford Centre for Staff Development.

Williams K (1996). *Essential writing skills*. Developing writing series. Oxford: Oxford Centre for Staff Development.

Useful sources

Learnhigher (2009). Critical thinking and reflection resources page. Available at http://www.learnhigher.ac.uk/learningareas/criticalthinkingandreflection/resourcepage.htm
  This list is carefully selected and regularly updated. Worth an explore.

University of Manchester (2005). Academic phrasebank. Available at: http://www.phrasebank.manchester.ac.uk/index.htm [Accessed 6 February 2009].
  Designed for academic writers in general, it is a superb resource for anyone looking for words and phrases to use in their writing. It is user friendly, well organised, and well worth exploring.

Wirral University Teaching Hospital (no date). *Evaluating web resources.* Library Helpsheet No 8. Available at: http://www.whnt.nhs.uk/document_uploads/Library_Services/Helpsheet [Accessed 8 November 2008].
  This 2-side pdf guide to evaluating web sources uses a different framework (Relevance, Authority, Objectivity, Accuracy). It is aimed at healthcare students but useful to anyone.

Index

action plan, 5–6
analyse, 9, 13, 66, 72, 79–81
annotated bibliography, 37–9
answer the question, 44–8
apply, xi, 13, 75
argument, 9, 10, 49, 66, 68
assessment, 7–12

bibliography, 37

compare, 13, 73
conclusion, 10–11
course handbook, 2–3
critical analysis, 7, 10, 44–7, 66, 77–86
critical thinking, 12–13, 62–4, 87
'critical' meaning, viii–xi

describe, 11, 13, 70–1

essay questions, 45–7
evaluate, xi, 7, 13, 32, 39, 74

evidence, ix, 9, 11, 62, 64, 66

feedback, vii, 9–11, 65–6
frameworks, 77–87

grades, 9–11, 14
groupwork, 82–4

implications, 34–6, 76

journal articles, 18–21
justify, 13, 76, 87

keywords, 24, 27

learning outcomes, 3
library, 22–7

notes, 30–1

online searching, 22–7

paragraphs, 49–60
peer-reviewed, 21, 66

questions, ask, viii, 1, 25–6, 33–6, 45–7, 64

reading, 9, 17–21, 26–8, 29
reference, 18–20, 30–1, 35, 39–40
reflection, 39, 82–6
research, 9, 17, 22–8, 66

so what? 27, 34–6, 54–7, 62
strategic questions, 1, 26, 33–6
summary, 39, 67
SWOT, 79–81
synthesise, 13, 41, 43, 67, 73

team roles, 82–4
textbooks, 18, 19, 21
timeline, 6, 89
topic sentence, 50–4, 67

URL, 33

voice, 61–4

website, 20, 21, 32–6
writing, 4, 61–4, 66–8, 88

POCKET STUDY SKILLS
Kate Williams & Jude Carroll

REFERENCING
& UNDERSTANDING
PLAGIARISM

POCKET STUDY SKILLS
Sue Robbins
SCIENCE STUDY SKILLS

STUDY SKILLS
...us
BRILLIANT WRITING TIPS FOR STUDENTS

PLANNING YOUR ESSAY

POCKET STUD...
...net Godwin

POCKET STUDY SKILLS
Andy Pulman
BLOGS WIKIS PODCASTS & MORE